a book of
simple pleasures

a book of
simple pleasures

Leigh Crandall

RYLAND
PETERS
& SMALL

LONDON NEW YORK

SENIOR DESIGNER Toni Kay
COMMISSIONING EDITOR
Annabel Morgan
PICTURE RESEARCH Emily Westlake
PRODUCTION Toby Marshall
ART DIRECTOR Leslie Harrington
PUBLISHING DIRECTOR Alison Starling

First published in 2011 by
Ryland Peters & Small
20–21 Jockey's Fields
London WC1R 4BW
and
519 Broadway, Fifth Floor
New York, NY 10012
www.rylandpeters.com

Text copyright ©
Leigh Crandall 2011
Design and commissioned
photography copyright
© Ryland Peters & Small 2011

10 9 8 7 6 5 4 3 2 1

ISBN 978-1-84975-139-1
Printed and bound in China.

contents

It is always the simple that produces the marvelous.

AMELIA BARR

introduction

There's a lot going on these days: social media, mobile devices, streaming movies, downloading music, 24-hour news, email, Facebook, TV, MP3, Wii, PSP. Phew! That's a ton of stimulation, and that isn't the half of it.

I'm not suggesting that we chuck it all and go back to a bygone era of oil lamps and sending mail via horse messenger. In fact, some of the ideas you'll find in this book employ modern technology. My point is that, with all we have in front of us these days, it can be easy to forget life's most elementary pleasures; to stop and smell the roses as it were. And this is a loss because, even with all our amazing inventions, it's still the simple things that bring us the greatest satisfaction and sense of well-being.

What follows is a collection of inspiring quotes, easy ideas for good living, and stories from real people about simple things they do that enrich their lives. As I write this little book from the plushy chair in the nook of my bedroom where I spend countless hours reading (one of my own simple pleasures), my hope is that the ideas and anecdotes within these pages will bring a smile to your face, maybe give you a good idea or two, and serve as a reminder that when we stop to enjoy the beauty of everyday things— particularly the simple ones—our lives inevitably become richer.

Leigh Crandall

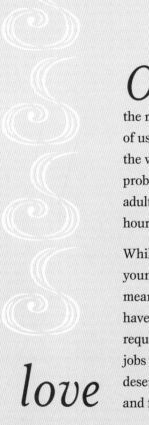

love

Oliver Wendell Holmes said, "Life is a romantic business, but you have to make the romance." It's a good point, really. Many of us remember our youth as the period when the world seemed most romantic, and that's probably because, when we lived without adult responsibilities, we simply had more hours and energy to devote to our relationships.

While we may never be as carefree as the younger versions of ourselves, this doesn't mean we have to sacrifice romance. We just have to make time for each other. We're required to show up and do our best at our jobs on a regular basis, and our relationships deserve the same. It's our wealth of family and friends that matters most after all.

*"The supreme happiness of life is
the conviction that we are loved."*

VICTOR HUGO

*"Friends are the thermometer by which we may judge
the temperature of our fortunes."*

LADY MARGUERITE BLESSINGTON

*"Families are like fudge—
mostly sweet with a few nuts."*

ANONYMOUS

*"To get the full value of a joy, you must have
somebody to divide it with."*

MARK TWAIN

*"My only sketch, profile, of heaven is a large blue sky, and larger than the biggest
I have seen in June—and in it are my friends—every one of them."*

EMILY DICKINSON

"The company makes the feast."

ANONYMOUS

"Friend: One who knows all about you and loves you just the same."

ELBERT HUBBARD

"A friend may well be reckoned the masterpiece of nature."

RALPH WALDO EMERSON

"Of all the things which wisdom provides to make life entirely happy, much the greatest is the possession of friendship."

EPICURUS

"We cannot live only for ourselves. A thousand fibers connect us with our fellow men."

HERMAN MELVILLE

"The loving are the daring."

BAYARD TAYLOR

"We cannot destroy kindred: our chains stretch a little sometimes, but they never break."

MARQUISE DE SÉVIGNÉ

"As in the case of wines that improve with age, the oldest friendship ought to be the most delightful."

CICERO

" In the kitchen at my husband's family summer house in Maine, there's a shelf full of black and white notebooks. His grandmother kept a page for every dinner she hosted at the house, listing what she served as well as the guests. At Thanksgiving, we love to flip through the books, which read like a portrait of the family in food over several decades. You can even pinpoint the first time his mother brought his father to dinner in the 1970s. Although I only met his grandmother in the last years of her life, her notebooks make me feel like I know her better...and I get a great kick out of seeing how the meals changed over the years. " *Sarah*

simple idea

For an inexpensive gift everyone will love, compile all your family recipes into one spot. Ask everyone in your extended family to contribute new dishes they've grown to love, as well as recipes that have become family traditions. Collect them together in a book and illustrate with copies of family photos; or print recipes on index cards and house them in recipe boxes—one for each family.

“On my mother's 75th birthday, she bought herself a beautiful tiara to wear for the weekend of festivities. She had such fun with it that she decided to start a "sisterhood," in which the tiara would be sent to other women to wear when they celebrated their own special occasions. The tiara travels with a photo album to which each woman adds a photo of herself wearing the tiara at her event. So far, the tiara has been to Florida, New York, Vermont, the Bahamas, the Virgin Islands, and Mexico, and has adorned the heads of mothers, daughters, nieces, and friends who celebrated special events from birthdays and anniversaries to graduations and bridal showers.” *Dawn*

simple idea

Keep a bound daily planner, even if you use an electronic calendar to manage your day-to-day life. By quickly jotting down the little events from your day, you'll have an easy-to-reference record of past weeks and months. Glance at it before you get on the phone or head out to dinner to catch up with friends and family. This way, when someone asks, "What have you been up to?" you'll have the highlights from the time that's passed between conversations top of your mind. And, most planners also have a "notes" section—a handy place to jot down lists of books you read, movies you've seen, and places you've visited throughout the year.

❝Shortly after my husband and I started our family, we were transferred and couldn't get to our parents' homes for Christmas for the first time since we'd been married. I wanted the holiday to be memorable, so I made a special meal on Christmas Eve and turned off all the lights so that only candles lit the house. Spending Christmas Eve in candlelight became an annual tradition. The first Christmas my oldest son was away, he even sent a beautiful oil lamp that was marked "to be opened on Christmas Eve." I love the peaceful, festive feeling candlelight gives a house, and without distractions like television, everyone is more apt to enjoy the evening talking and celebrating and together.❞ *Dianne*

simple idea

You don't have to save candlelight for special occasions and romantic dinners à deux. Embrace its calming effect by taking a few hours once or twice a month to unplug, light a few candles, and enjoy the tranquility of the soft light on your own.

"When I was first married, my husband and I were living in a modest house, with modest means, and I never felt I could host guests at the level I wanted to. So I didn't. One night, at an event thrown by a friend who loved entertaining, I confessed that I longed to hold parties myself, but felt I couldn't if they weren't of a certain caliber. She insisted that throwing a great party was about thoughtful touches...not fancy food, wine, or surroundings.

I've thrown a lot of parties since then and, heeding my friend's advice, my focus is always on my guests and what would make them most comfortable. For family, it's either a casual meal like a barbeque, or a holiday feast. I cook something new or make an old favourite. When a new recipe works, it's a success, if it flops we have a good laugh, and when I make something tried and true, it becomes part of family tradition. I tend to host groups of friends in the summer. I keep the menu simple and we eat outdoors on the patio—there's something about eating al fresco that puts everyone at ease. Paired with good music and wine, it's always fun.

My advice is this: Keep things simple and relaxed. It's not a contest. And enjoy yourself—if you have fun, then your guests will, too! " *Debbie*

easy entertaining ideas:

A Fondue "Do" It's inexpensive, delicious, and interactive—helpful for breaking the ice with guests who don't know each other well and fun for those who do.

Homemade Pizza Party Have guests add ingredients to their own pizza. For added fun, make your own dough and let guests toss it in the air.

Cocktail Swap Ask each to guest to bring the ingredients for a drink recipe that incorporates the same type of alcohol (e.g. everyone would bring a recipe for a gin-based cocktail) and vote on whose concoction tastes the best.

Posh Picnic Organize a get-together in a local park or, even easier, in your own backyard. Ask everyone to bring their own picnic blanket and a dish to share. Dress it up with real plates, utensils, and glassware (instead of plastic).

Ugly Sweater Ball The goal of this party is for everyone to come dressed in the least-attractive sweater possible. It's an easy theme to pull off, and also one that provides an instant conversation-starter.

" When my husband and I go on a long car trip, I bring books. He drives, and I read out loud. It's easy to zone out in the car, but reading keeps us engaged and talking, and experiencing something new together. We arrive at our destination with all sorts of new jokes about what we've read. There are other benefits, too: If it's a page turner, we actually look forward to the long drive home, and if we don't finish the book on the trip, shorter drives can transport us back to a recent vacation. My favorite books for car reading are classics—we just finished *Alice in Wonderland*. To make sure you're both into the book, bring several options and read the first page of each out loud, then let the other person pick. " *Emily*

car games to play together

"I'm Going to Grandma's House" Each person begins their turn with the phrase, "I'm going to grandma's house, and I'm taking…" then says the name of an item. The next player must recite every item listed, and add another. To make it easier for younger players, follow the alphabet. Players are out when they're unable to recall an item on the list, and the last player to recite the whole list wins.

The Last Word Players take turns reciting lines from popular songs. The person with the first turn sings one line (for example: "All You Need is Love"), then the next player must think of a line from another song that incorporates the last word from the previous line (in this case, "love"). If you're unable to think of a line you're out. The last player to successfully recite lyrics using the word given by the previous player wins.

"Once Upon a Time" Great for kids, in this game the group creates an original story as each player takes turns adding one line at a time. The first player starts with the phrase, "Once upon a time". The second player then adds another line to the story, the third another, and so on, until the story naturally reaches an end. So long as the new line references the last one, players can take the story in any direction they want—the sillier the better.

❝Years ago, my mother started emailing her five grandchildren every Monday morning with her words of wisdom to begin their week (we called it "Monday's WOW!"). In these emails, she'd share her thoughts on a wide variety of topics —dating, driving, ethics, friendship, and whatever else she felt was important— and the kids would write back with their thoughts on the subject, too.

This simple act kept her in touch with her grandkids as they grew up, and it has given them something to reflect upon as they go through their busy lives in school and college. She's been amazed at the impact that it has made in their lives, as well as her own. She's saved all her emails to them, as well as their responses, and recently gave each grandchild a personal album with copies of their correspondence so they'll always have them.❞ *Dawn*

simple idea

Many of us store our photos digitally now—it's handy for organization purposes—but nothing beats flipping through a photo album. For a sweet gift for close friends and relatives, use a bookmaking website (like Blurb or iPhoto) to create a small "greatest hits" album of your family's photos from the year. The programs are easy to use, and you can simply drag and drop photos in and type in captions—much less time consuming than placing each into an album by hand, and you can order multiple copies.

"We all go through that stage of adolescence when it seems everything our parents do is an embarrassment. When I was about ten years old, my mother thought it would be 'cute' to dress the whole family in matching flannel shirts and have us take a family picture. At the time, I was mortified to be seen dressed the same as my parents (and photographic evidence was even worse!).

Nearly 20 years later, I found my father's flannel shirt from that day, had a laugh with my mom over it, and claimed the shirt for myself. That shirt has been a source of comfort to me ever since. It was the piece of clothing I chose to wear one night when a major hurricane threatened my home and I thought I might have to evacuate with only the clothes on my back. I still have it, and my dad's shirt continues to provide me with the same sense of comfort and well-being he always did." *Cindy*

simple idea

Most of us have articles of clothing (either our own or ones that remind us of loved ones) that we could never part with. Rather than keeping them in a box, consider putting them to practical use and having a quilt made from their fabric or framing them in an artful way. Not that crafty? Check out etsy.com—home to all things handmade—to find an artisan who can create one for you.

We've all heard the phrase "carpe diem". The popular translation, "seize the day," is usually taken as a suggestion for the present (e.g. get off the couch and go out and enjoy the beautiful weather). This saying doesn't just refer to how you choose to spend the hour at hand, though. It's also about making choices that will allow you to build a future that's ripe with possibilities. Whether it's something big, like your relationships, or something small, like taking the time to make yourself a proper meal, "carpe diem" is about becoming a person of action. It's about making space for what you love and striving to change things you don't like. By seizing the day, you make steps towards shaping your life into one that's more representative of the person you are, and the satisfaction of a day well-lived is one of the greatest pleasures of all.

live

"Light tomorrow with today."

ELIZABETH BARRETT BROWNING

"Character is simply habit long enough continued."

JOSEPH CONRAD

"It is neither wealth nor splendor, but tranquility and occupation which give happiness."

THOMAS JEFFERSON

"Always bear in mind that your own resolution to success is more important than any other one thing."

ABRAHAM LINCOLN

"Never put off until tomorrow what you can do today, because if you enjoy it today, you can do it again tomorrow."

ANONYMOUS

"Well done is better than well said."

BENJAMIN FRANKLIN

"Happiness is an expression of the soul in considered actions."

ARISTOTLE

"No matter what looms ahead, if you can eat today, enjoy the sunlight today, mix good cheer with friends today, enjoy it and bless God for it."

HENRY WARD BEECHER

66 Most days I wake up a couple of hours before my two boys so I can exercise and clear my head. This time in the morning is "my time". Taking a small amount of time just for myself not only keeps me fit, but also sane, which allows me to be a better mom and a better wife. Living in balance makes me appreciate what I have, and I count my blessings every day. 99 *Andrea*

simple thought

66 Have regular hours for work and play; make each day both useful and pleasant, and prove that you understand the worth of time by employing it well. Then youth will be delightful, old age will bring few regrets, and life will become a beautiful success. 99

LOUISA MAY ALCOTT

66 Growing up in the country with green-thumbed parents meant that having fresh flowers on the table wasn't a luxury but simply a part of our daily life. When guests came to stay, my mother would send me out to the garden to put a few blooms in an antique bottle she had salvaged from a junk shop. She would place the flowers on their bedside table and I was always amazed at the profound effect such a simple gesture could have on a room. The joy and life that even the simplest of arrangements can bring to a space is extraordinary. 99 *Juliet of Poppies & Posies*

66 Although there is an undeniable beauty in arranged flowers for a special occasion such as a wedding or a dinner party, there is something so charming about having fresh flowers in the house "just because." As a floral designer and event planner, most people think my house and office would be filled with extravagant arrangements, but the truth is I like nothing more than going to the farmers markets on the weekend and buying a bunch of whatever local wildflowers are available. I keep old glass jars around the house and fill them with whatever blooms I picked up that day. The un-arranged beauty of wildflowers can brighten up any space. 99
Sierra of Poppies & Posies

simple idea

Fresh flower arrangements don't have to be extravagant in size or housed in a fancy vase. Flea-market finds such as colored-glass bottles or wooden cigar boxes make charming vessels and add vintage flair to a modest arrangement. If containers are on the small side, group several together in one spot to make more of an impact.

" When I moved to New York City, I was looking for a release. I wanted some time to myself, to think or not to think; to just be. I wasn't sure if running would be the answer, but once I started, I found a whole new side of myself that I didn't know existed. When I started to run, I couldn't even go a mile; and now I've run a marathon. Running can be challenging, but the people I've met through the sport, the places I've explored, and the things I've achieved have made every step worth it. " *Lisa*

25 songs to jumpstart your workout

UNDER PRESSURE, by David Bowie and Queen ❀ PON DE REPLAY, by Rihanna

RAY OF LIGHT, by Madonna ❀ SUPERSTITION, by Stevie Wonder

DANCING IN THE DARK, by Bruce Springsteen

YOU SHOOK ME ALL NIGHT LONG, by AC/DC

DON'T STOP BELIEVIN', by Journey ❀ MY SHARONA, by The Knack

YEAH, by Usher ❀ HOT-N-FUN, by N.E.R.D. featuring Nelly Furtado

BAMBOLEO, by the Gipsy Kings ❀ I'M A BELIEVER, by the Monkees

JUMP (FOR MY LOVE), by The Pointer Sisters ❀ TAKE ON ME, by A-ha

EVERYDAY, by the Dave Matthews Band ❀ DANCING WITH MYSELF, by Billy Idol

DON'T LEAVE ME THIS WAY, by Thelma Houston

DANCING QUEEN by ABBA ❀ JUMP, by Van Halen

MAGIC CARPET RIDE, by Steppenwolf ❀ YOU WRECK ME, by Tom Petty

THE WAY YOU MAKE ME FEEL, AND WANNA BE STARTING SOMETHING,
by Michael Jackson

D'YER MAK'ER, by Led Zepplin ❀ I WILL FOLLOW, by U2

simple idea

The majority of the human body is composed of water. It only
makes sense that this liquid is a great source of joy and comfort
to many of us, yet so many of us go a long time without
experiencing some of the simple pleasures it provides. When
was the last time you…

❀ went skinny-dipping

❀ took a long, hot bath

❀ lay in a cozy spot and listened to the sound of rain
hitting the roof

❀ stood at the edge of the ocean and gazed out to sea

❀ passionately kissed someone in the rain

❀ watched fish swim around an aquarium (or even better,
went diving or snorkeling)

❀ listened to the sound of running water, like a stream or
brook, or listened to waves crashing upon a shore

❀ took a boat out onto a body of water and watched
the sunset

❀ stopped to breathe in the smell of rain

❀ jumped in a puddle

simple idea

Create an inspiration board. It doesn't have to be an oversized collage, just something to offer a daily reminder of your dreams and passions. It should include your goals and aspirations (a photo of the spot you're hoping to live or a trip you want to take), and also things you've achieved that you're proud of. Keep it somewhere you can see it every morning. A quick glance at the accomplishments of your past and your dreams for the future can be a great motivator.

simple thought

66 Three grand essentials
to happiness in this life
are something to do,
something to love, and
something to hope for. 99

JOSEPH ADDISON

simple thought

"I am not afraid of storms,
for I am learning how to sail
my ship."

LOUISA MAY ALCOTT

ideas to lift your mood

Rediscover your cookbooks Online recipes are handy, but they rarely have the beautiful photos, wonderful stories, and wine pairing suggestions found in a good cookbook. Tab pages that inspire you—it will get you excited about cooking again.

Bake something Even if it's just ready-made cookie dough, the aroma of baked goods is always heavenly.

Get moving Exercise stimulates chemicals in your brain that leave you feeling more relaxed and happier post-workout, so go for a walk, do some yoga, or put on some music and dance!

Pick up the phone and call someone It can be easy to fall into reading people's Facebook updates, but nothing replaces hearing the news directly from a friend or family member.

Make a plan Be proactive and propose a get-together with friends so that you'll have a social event to look forward to.

Go see something beautiful Head out to a garden or park and treat yourself to the sight of some gorgeous natural scenery, or to a museum for some artistic stimulation. It beats whiling away the hours in front of reality television.

Take a deep breath A few minutes of concentrated, deep breathing can help relieve anxiety.

comforting things you should always have at home

POPCORN ❀ HOT COCOA OR TEA ❀ YOUR FAVOURITE SWEET TREAT

A PAIR OF SUPERSNUG PAJAMAS ❀ WOOL SOCKS

A DOWN BLANKET ❀ A PLAYLIST OF SONGS YOU FIND COMFORTING

CANDLES ❀ YOUR TOP 10 FILMS

feel-good films

FERRIS BUELLER'S DAY OFF ❀ PRIDE AND PREJUDICE ❀ GROUNDHOG DAY

WAKING NED DEVINE ❀ THE PRINCESS BRIDE ❀ WHEN HARRY MET SALLY

BRIDGET JONES'S DIARY ❀ LOVE ACTUALLY ❀ NOTTING HILL ❀ FATHER OF THE BRIDE

PRETTY WOMAN ❀ SLIDING DOORS ❀ THE SOUND OF MUSIC ❀ DIRTY DANCING

SHAKESPEARE IN LOVE ❀ GREASE ❀ RUDY ❀ MY BIG FAT GREEK WEDDING

simple thought

"There is nothing like staying at home for real comfort."

JANE AUSTEN

simple thought

"Oh bed! Oh bed! Delicious bed!
That heaven on earth to the weary head!"

THOMAS HOOD

simple idea

A good night's sleep is a simple pleasure we can all agree on. For the most rejuvenating rest, the American Academy of Sleep Medicine recommends that you:

❀ Avoid caffeine, alcohol, nicotine, heavy meals, and exercising prior to bedtime

❀ Don't go to bed unless you're sleepy. Instead, find something to do that will relax you (like reading a magazine or listening to soft music) so that you're not worried about falling asleep

❀ Eat a small snack before bedtime to avoid going to sleep hungry

❀ Signal to your body that it's bedtime by avoiding bright lights at night

❀ Follow a consistent bedtime routine that includes rituals that help you relax (like a warm bath or a few minutes of reading)

❀ Make your bedroom quiet, dark, and cool

❀ Avoid taking naps

❀ Keep a regular schedule for meals, chores, medications, and other daily activities to keep your inner body clock running smoothly

❀ Get up at the same time every morning

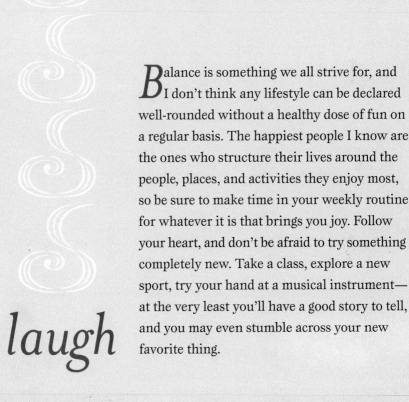

laugh

*B*alance is something we all strive for, and I don't think any lifestyle can be declared well-rounded without a healthy dose of fun on a regular basis. The happiest people I know are the ones who structure their lives around the people, places, and activities they enjoy most, so be sure to make time in your weekly routine for whatever it is that brings you joy. Follow your heart, and don't be afraid to try something completely new. Take a class, explore a new sport, try your hand at a musical instrument— at the very least you'll have a good story to tell, and you may even stumble across your new favorite thing.

"Love, and do what you will."

SAINT AUGUSTINE

*"We live in an ascending scale when we live happily,
one thing leading to another in an endless series."*

ROBERT LOUIS STEVENSON

*"Enjoy yourself, drink, call the life you live today your
own—but only that; the rest belongs to chance."*

EURIPIDES

*"The most thoroughly wasted of all days is that
on which one has not laughed."*

NICOLAS DE CHAMFORT

"A well-spent day brings happy sleep."

LEONARDO DA VINCI

*"When love and skill work together,
expect a masterpiece."*

JOHN RUSKIN

"Come, let us give a little time to folly…and even in a melancholy day let us find time for an hour of pleasure."

SAINT BONAVENTURA

"One hour of life, crowded to the full with glorious action and filled with noble risks, is worth whole years of those mean observances of paltry decorum."

SIR WALTER SCOTT

"There is no cosmetic for beauty like happiness."

LADY MARGUERITE BLESSINGTON

"Happiness consists in the full employment of our faculties in some pursuit."

HARRIET MARTINEAU

"The really happy person is one who can enjoy the scenery on a detour."

ANONYMOUS

simple idea

If you yearn to travel but can't do so as often as you like, become a tourist in your own town. Don't wait until guests come to visit to go out and explore your local attractions, festivals, dramatic productions, art galleries, and music venues. Make a list of all of the spots you'd like to see within a day's drive of your home, too, and visit them in between longer trips.

"I love to travel, and I try to do so as inexpensively as possible so I can see more places for longer periods of time. My mom is always asking me why I feel the need to run off to foreign lands, and I've asked myself the same question many times, especially when I have struggled to find comfort on a metal bench in a dark bus station or while haggling with a taxi driver who I know is ripping me off. Every time, the answer is always the same: I travel because I am curious, because it makes me feel free and alive, and because the surprises and adventures I've had in foreign lands have humbled my views and expanded my mind. When I travel, I'm forced to ask myself who I am without the tapestry of my family, my friends, my job, my food, my language, and my obligations. Ultimately, I explain to my mom, I travel to discover a new sense of home." *Katie*

"There's nothing more relaxing than a glass of wine paired with some great music. The pace of the day usually decides my playlist. I like a wide variety of music, and many times I'll just play my favorite song from each of the albums I've collected over the years. At the end of a more taxing day, I settle down to my collection of movie scores. Add a Zinfandel or Cabernet and a comfy chair to listen in, and it doesn't get much better." *Marc*

simple idea

Most of us have extensive music collections, but there's just something about hearing a song you love out of the blue that beats having it at your fingertips. Check out free internet radio stations such as Last.fm, where you can enter a musician or a song you like and tunes by similar artists will play continuously. Or choose one of the site's preset stations by genre (i.e. "hip hop"). It's a great way to stumble across old favorites, as well as discover new music. Here are some artists you might want to try:

For oldies you can sing along to: DION

For the best of the blues: RAY CHARLES

For classic country crooning: DOLLY PARTON OR JOHNNY CASH

For upbeat, pop hits from the 80s: HALL & OATES

For new music with a classic rock sound: THE BLACK KEYS

For mellow, modern folk: IRON & WINE OR JOSÉ GONZALEZ

For sexy R&B: MARVIN GAYE OR AL GREEN

For air guitar sessions: VAN HALEN

For 90s grunge nostalgia: NIRVANA

For vintage jazz: BILLIE HOLIDAY OR ART TATUM

“ Shopping certainly isn't the most virtuous pastime, but like a nibble of chocolate here or a nip of good whiskey there, the act of shopping can be enjoyed in moderation. Studies have shown that shopping releases endorphins, so there's even a little science to back up my claims that wandering into a new boutique, rummaging through the shelves of a used bookstore, or examining curios in the aisles of a flea market offer more than a few happy-making benefits.

The fact is, you don't even have to spend a lot to reap the benefits of shopping. While stocking up on sundries at my local drug store, I delight in new beauty products, and read their labels with interest. And the travel-size products—you can never have too many of these tiny, fairy-sized treats.

Some other guilt-free shopping haunts include farmer's markets (how could an armful of rainbow-colored zinnias, and luscious heirloom tomatoes be considered a waste of money?); pet supply stores (there is often a resident cat to coo at); and antique stores, where gilded mirrors and crystal chandeliers fan the flames of my imagination in such a vivid way, it's almost like reading a novel. ” *Amy Elliott, author of* A Girl's Guide to Retail Therapy

simple idea

Sick of your clothes? Get several friends together and host a clothes swapping evening, where everyone brings items they're willing to trade—it's a fun, easy way to acquire new clothes without spending money!

fifteen simple pleasures from childhood you should try again:

❀ Go as high as you can on a swing, then jump off

❀ Walk barefoot on grass

❀ Eat a meal made for a lunch box—a simple sandwich (like peanut butter and jelly), your favorite fruit, pudding, and chocolate milk

❀ Spend hours playing board games and cards on a rainy day

❀ Have a no-holds-barred air-guitar session

❀ Throw a themed birthday party

❀ Climb a tree

❀ Do a cartwheel

❀ Organize a group game like Capture the Flag or Touch Football

❀ Make up a dance routine to a favorite song

❀ Run downhill at a sprint

❀ Ride a bike (without it being about "getting a workout")

❀ Build a sand castle

❀ Have a water-balloon fight

❀ Try to catch fireflies at dusk on a warm, summer evening

"I've been making jewelry for many years now. I began with simple designs and have graduated to more complex pieces. Having the ability to make something beautiful not only gives me great pleasure, but a real sense of pride—watching my ideas slowly develop into an incredible piece is an amazing thing! There's nothing more gratifying than knowing you used your creativity to make something that someone will cherish." *Rachel*

simple thought

"Every artist was first an amateur."

RALPH WALDO EMERSON

"Sitting at work, all I can think is 'I'd rather be knitting'. On a workday, the most knitting I get to do is on the subway on the way to and from work, and sometimes, I wish I could stay on the train past my stop so I can continue knitting. Every time I knit in public, and especially when I knit on the subway, someone asks me about it. I've met the most amazing people because of knitting.

A knitter knows what goes into making a sock or a sweater, mittens or a hat. Every finished garment has a world of experience behind it. And every day, there are new ways to knit that people are discovering and sharing. Knitters share what they know; I've never met a selfish knitter. I love that I'm part of this grand tapestry of creative people that's rich with history and continues to grow, one knitter at a time." *Michelle*

simple idea

Book clubs are a great idea for friends who love to read. But some people feel stressed by the idea of having to finish a book by a certain deadline. So, think outside the box for clubs you might want to start. Compelling magazine articles, short stories, or essays are other ideas for readers. Or revolve get-togethers around food—each meeting might feature nibbles from different parts of the world, for example, or simple pairings, like dessert and wine or tacos and margaritas. Music-lovers might meet up and take turns playing songs from a new artist they've discovered, or you can theme the night by genre or decade and have each person bring their top three songs to play.

66 My husband Josh and I have always enjoyed camping. We're both nature lovers, and over the years, the times we've spent in the outdoors have been some of our favorites—Josh even proposed to me at the top of a mountain. For me, the natural beauty of this planet is a spiritual thing—being surrounded by nature is a reminder that I'm a part of something so much bigger than myself. Plus, camping isn't expensive, so we can go whenever we like. Being away from everyday life and getting outside keeps my husband and I connected, and we have so many wonderful memories from our trips. Now that we have a daughter, I can't wait to share the beauty of nature with her, and make new memories as a family, too. 99 *Kristin*

simple thought

66 Simplicity is the ultimate sophistication. 99

LEONARDO DI VINCI

simple idea

Camping forces everyone out of their day-to-day routine and, without the distraction of modern amenities, you're free to bond over the simple adventure that comes with sleeping outside. If you aren't sure the wilderness is for you, try pitching a tent in your own backyard and set the mood with:

TOASTED MARSHMALLOWS
(use a grill if you don't want to start
a campfire)

❧

GHOST STORIES

❧

CAMP SONGS

❧

THERMOS FLASKS OF COFFEE
OR HOT CHOCOLATE

❧

SLEEPING BAGS

❧

STAR GAZING

Acknowledgments

I would like to thank everyone who contributed their wonderful ideas and stories to this book, particularly my friends and family. Thanks also to Alison Starling and Annabel Morgan at Ryland Peters & Small for their help and support on this project and to mom, dad, Dale, and Chris for providing me with the simple pleasure of knowing I am loved.

Picture Credits

Key: ph = photographer, a = above, b = below, r = right, l = left, c = center.

Page 1 ph Polly Wreford/the home in Denmark of Charlotte Gueniau of RICE (www.rice.dk); 2 ph Debi Treloar; 3 ph Jonathan Gregson; 4–5 ph Polly Wreford/Foster House available to hire through www.beachstudios.co.uk; 6 ph Debi Treloar/available for location hire at www.shootspaces.com; 7 ph Kate Whitaker; 8 ph Catherine Gratwicke/Victoria Davar and Shane Meredith of Maison Artefact (www.maisonartefact.com); 10–11 Image taken from Japanese Patterns, published by The Pepin Press, www.pepinpress.com; 12–13 ph Kate Whitaker; 14ph Daniel Farmer; 15 ph Polly Wreford; 16 ph Sandra Lane; 17 ph Winfried Heinze; 18 ph Caroline Arber; 20 ph Polly Wreford/Paul & Claire's beach house, East Sussex. Design: www.davecoote.com; Location hire: www.beachstudios.co.uk; 22 ph Debi Treloar/Khadi & Co. by Bess Nielsen khadiandco@hotmail.com;

23 ph Paul Massey/the home in Denmark of Charlotte Lynggaard, designer of Ole Lynggaard Copenhagen www.olelynggaard.dk; 24 ph Kate Whitaker; 25 ph Jan Baldwin/owner of Girl's Own Store, Sara Mahon's cottage in West Dorset www.girlsownstore.co.uk; 26 ph Catherine Gratwicke/Charlotte-Anne Fidler and Matthew Griffiths www.airspaces.co.uk; 28–29 Image taken from Japanese Patterns, published by The Pepin Press, www.pepinpress.com; 30l ph Debi Treloar; 30c ph Jan Bladwin; 30r ph Winfried Heinze; 31 ph Polly Wreford/Foster House available to hire through www.beachstudios.co.uk; 32 ph Polly Wreford; 33 ph Polly Wreford; 34 ph Chris Everard; 36 ph Polly Wreford/the home in Lewes of Justin & Heidi Francis, owner of Flint, www.flintcollection.com; 37 ph Paul Massey; 38 ph Debi Treloar/ceramicist Jette Arendal Winther's home in Denmark, www.arendal-ceramics.com; 39 ph Debi Treloar/the home of Julia Bird in Cornwall www.birdkids.co.uk; 40 ph Kate Whitaker; 42 l&c ph Jonathan Gregson; 42r ph Polly Wreford; 43 ph Polly Wreford/www.beachstudios.co.uk; 44 ph Catherine Gratwicke/Sue A'Court (www.suewilliamsacourt.co.uk); 46 ph Claire Richardson; 48–49 Image taken from Japanese Patterns, published by The Pepin Press, www.pepinpress.com; 50 ph Caroline Arber/designed and made by Jane Cassini and Ann Brownfield; 51 ph Paul Massey; 52 ph Mark Scott; 55 ph Debi Treloar/The home of Isobel Trenouth, her husband and their four children available through www.shootspaces.com; 56 ph Chris Everard; 58–60 ph Claire Richardson; 61 ph James Merrell; 63 ph Polly Wreford/the family home of Sarah and Mark Benton in Rye (www.lionstreetstore.co.uk).

64